KU-132-423

Earthquakes

Tami Deedrick

Raintree

Nature on the Rampage

www.raintreepublishers.co.uk

Visit our website to find out more information about **Raintree** books.

To order:
☎ Phone 44 (0) 1865 8880112
▤ Send a fax to 44 (0) 1865 314091
▱ Visit the Raintree Bookshop at www.raintreepublishers.co.uk to browse our catalogue and order online.

First published in Great Britain by Raintree Publishers, Halley Court, Jordan Hill, Oxford, OX2 8EJ, part of Harcourt Education.
Raintree is a registered trademark of Harcourt Education Ltd.

Content Consultant: Stuart Sipkin, Geophysicist, United States Geological Survey

Editorial: Kate Buckingham and Isabel Thomas
Cover design: Jo Sapwell
(www.tipani.co.uk)
Production: Jonathan Smith

Originated by Dot Gradations
Printed and bound in China by South China Printing Company

ISBN 1 844 21211 4
07 06 05 04 03
10 9 8 7 6 5 4 3 2 1

British Library Cataloguing in Publication Data
Deedrick, Tami
Earthquakes. - Nature on the Rampage
1.Earthquakes - Juvenile literature
I.Title
551.2'2
A full catalogue for this book is available from the British Library

Acknowledgements
The publishers would like to thank the following for permission to reproduce photographs: Archive Photos, pp. **14–15**; Reuters/Cafer Esendemir, p. **22**; Reuters/R. Ezer, pp. **13, 24**; Reuters/Erik Ke Castro, p. **26**; National Oceanic and Atmospheric Administration, pp. **17, 18** (inset), **20, 21, 26**; Photo Network/Gay Bumgarner, p. **18**; Photophile, pp. **1, 4**; Visuals Unlimited/Doug Sokell, p. **9** (bottom).

Cover photograph by Rex Features

Every effort has been made to contact copyright holders of any material reproduced in this book. Any omissions will be rectified in subsequent printing if notice is given to the publishers.

Contents

When the Earth shakes

Many people believe the ground they stand on never moves. But the ground moves during earthquakes. It can shake or move like a wave of water. Earthquakes last from a few seconds to a few minutes.

Thousands of earthquakes happen every year. Most of these earthquakes are weak. A weak earthquake happens once every four days in the UK. But people do not feel weak earthquakes. Some earthquakes are strong. These destroy buildings and kill people. Earthquakes across the world have taken hundreds and thousands of lives in the last 100 years alone.

 A 1985 earthquake in Mexico destroyed thousands of buildings.

core

crust

Parts of the Earth

Movement of the layers that make up the Earth causes earthquakes. The core is the centre of the Earth. The mantle surrounds the core. The crust is the thin outer layer of the Earth. If the Earth were egg-sized, the crust would be as thick as the eggshell.

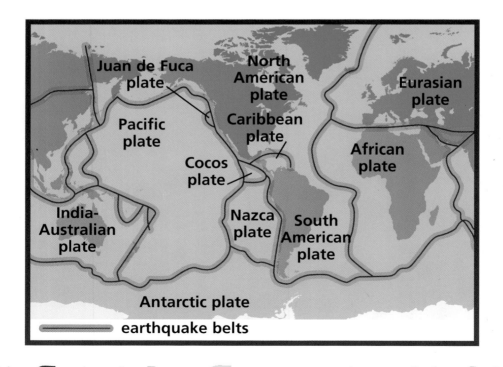

Juan de Fuca plate

North American plate

Eurasian plate

Pacific plate

Caribbean plate

African plate

Cocos plate

India-Australian plate

Nazca plate

South American plate

Antarctic plate

earthquake belts

Plates and earthquakes

Earthquakes can start in the Earth's mantle or crust. Sometimes earthquakes start when large rocks in the mantle move. But most earthquakes start in the crust.

Scientists think the crust is made up of large slabs of rock called **plates**, which move around on top of the molten mantle. No one is sure exactly how many plates there are. Some scientists think there are seven large plates and twelve smaller ones.

The plates move around very slowly, between 2.5 cm and 10 cm every year. Plates may move away from each other. They may also move past each other. Sometimes two plates stick as they move past each other. Pressure builds up until the plates suddenly slip and move quickly. This causes an earthquake.

Earthquakes can happen anywhere. But 90 per cent of earthquakes happen where plates meet. These places are called earthquake belts.

 This diagram shows the plates that make up the Earth's crust.

Earthquake damage

Earthquakes cause vibrations that can shake buildings, twist railway tracks and make bridges fall down. They can break gas pipes, which causes fires. Earthquakes can destroy **dams**, which causes floods. They can start landslides.

Damage is usually greatest near the **epicentre** of an earthquake. The epicentre is the part of the Earth's surface directly above the place where an earthquake starts. The shaking is usually stronger around the epicentre.

Earthquakes under water can start **tsunamis**. A tsunami is a series of huge waves that start in the ocean. Tsunamis can wash away buildings and drown people when they reach land.

Small earthquakes happen before and after large ones. **Foreshocks** are small earthquakes before a large one. **Aftershocks** are small earthquakes after a large one.

Big earthquakes do not always cause the most damage. The damage depends on how soft the ground is, how strong buildings are and how many people live in the area that is hit.

Earthquakes can cause fires (top) or floods (bottom).

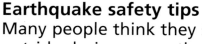

▲ **This block of flats was destroyed by the June 1998 earthquake in Turkey. People had to camp in tents outside the damaged building.**

Earthquake safety tips

Many people think they should run outside during an earthquake. Experts say this is wrong. You could get hurt by things falling on you. Instead, you should duck, cover and hold. Duck under a very heavy piece of furniture like a table. Take cover under something strong. Hold on to strong furniture once you have taken cover. Look for an open place if you are already outside. Stay away from buildings and electric wires. Stay in an open place until the shaking stops. Be prepared for aftershocks. Stay out of damaged buildings that could fall on you.

The Richter Scale

Charles Richter invented the **Richter Scale** in the 1930s. This scale measures the **magnitude**, or strength, of an earthquake by the size of the vibrations. Each number up the scale shows a ten times increase in strength. So a magnitude 7 earthquake is ten times more powerful than a magnitude 6. Most earthquakes are 1 or 2 on the Richter Scale. People cannot feel earthquakes of magnitude 1 or 2.

Description	Magnitude	Number a year
Great	8.0 or higher	1
Major	7.0 to 7.9	18
Strong	6.0 to 6.9	120
Moderate	5.0 to 5.9	800
Light	4.0 to 4.9	6200
Minor	3.0 to 3.9	49,000
Very minor	2.9 or lower	9000 every day

Earthquakes in history

People throughout history have told stories to explain why earthquakes happen because they did not know the scientific explanation. An old Native American story says a giant turtle carries the Earth on its back. Earthquakes happen when the turtle moves.

A story from ancient China says people live inside the Earth. Sometimes these people shake the ground. They do this to see if anyone outside is still living. The story says Chinese children should stamp their feet when they feel an earthquake and shout, 'Alive! Alive!' Then the people living inside the Earth will know the children are still alive.

This building in Mexico was destroyed by the huge 1985 earthquake.

▲ Most of the buildings in Tokyo and Yokohama were destroyed during the 1923 earthquakes.

Great Kanto Earthquake, Japan 1923

On 1 September 1923, an enormous earthquake hit two cities in Japan. It measured 8.3 on the **Richter Scale**.

The earthquake struck at lunchtime, when thousands of homes and restaurants had lit fires to prepare meals. Huge fires started. The earthquakes destroyed most of the buildings in Tokyo and Yokohama. Over 142,000 people died.

Chile, South America, 1960

The world's strongest recorded earthquake, measuring 9.5 on the Richter Scale, struck Chile on 22 May 1960. It started a tsunami that travelled across the Pacific Ocean, killing more people than the vibrations. Over 2000 people were killed as 10-metre waves flattened entire villages in Chile.

Several hours later, the tsunami had crossed the ocean to Hawaii, where it killed 61 people. Nearly 24 hours later, 140 people in Japan were killed by waves 8 metres high. Over 3000 people were injured and 2 million people made homeless by the combined effects of the tsunami and earthquake.

San Francisco, USA, 1906

Early in the morning of 18 April 1906, a large earthquake hit San Francisco, California. Scientists believe it was about 7.9 on the Richter Scale.

Huge cracks opened in the ground. Railway tracks twisted. Houses fell down. Many buildings were destroyed in parts of the city built on poor soil, which behaved like liquid when the vibrations passed through it.

But most of the damage was due to secondary causes. The earthquake broke gas pipes and made cookers fall over. Large fires started. The earthquake also broke water pipes. Firefighters had no water to fight the fires, which burned for days. In the end, dynamite was used to blow up buildings in the path of the fire so it ran out of fuel. About 30,000 buildings were destroyed.

The earthquake left about 200,000 people without homes. More than 3000 people died. Bridges, offices and roads in modern San Francisco have been built to stand up to earthquakes and prevent this tragedy happening again.

The 1906 San Francisco earthquake killed animals and destroyed many buildings.

In California, two plates meet along the San Andreas Fault (inset). Earthquakes happen when the plates move quickly.

Earthquakes today

An area that has many **faults** is a high-risk place for earthquakes. Faults are cracks in the Earth's crust. California in the USA has many faults. It also lies where two plates are moving past each other. The plates meet at the San Andreas Fault. This fault runs along almost the full length of California. Earthquakes happen around the San Andreas Fault as the plates move.

Movement along a fault in southern California caused an earthquake on 17 January 1994. It measured 6.7 on the **Richter Scale**. It damaged more than 100,000 buildings, cracked roads and destroyed bridges. The earthquake killed 57 people. Many lives were saved because the Californian authorities have good response and rescue times.

▲ **Parts of the main street in Anchorage sank.**

Anchorage, Alaska, 1964

On 28 March 1964, the strongest earthquake
ever to hit North America happened in Anchorage,
Alaska. The earthquake measured 9.2 on the
Richter Scale. It lasted three minutes and killed
131 people.

The earthquake broke roads into pieces. Bridges
fell into water. Large cracks opened in the ground.
A cinema sank 9 metres. Oil tanks used for fuel
exploded. The oil spilled into the ocean and began

▲ Tsunamis washed over Alaska's coasts.
A tsunami twisted these railway sleepers.

to burn. The earthquake also started a tsunami. Huge waves destroyed parts of Alaska's coast, carried boats on to land and destroyed buildings.

The strongest earthquake of 2002 happened in the same area of Alaska and measured 7.9 on the Richter Scale. This time, no one was killed.

Animals and earthquakes

Some people think animals can tell when an earthquake is coming. Animals may behave strangely before an earthquake. They might refuse to move or might become very active. Bears run out of their caves just before earthquakes. People have used tigers, snakes, horses, cats and dogs to tell when earthquakes are coming.

Turkey

The country of Turkey has a history of earthquakes because it sits on a small plate that is being squeezed between two huge plates. In 1939, an earthquake killed about 30,000 people there. Another earthquake hit Turkey in June 1998. It killed 144 people and injured over 1500.

In 1999, two major earthquakes shook the most crowded region of Turkey. Many buildings fell on top of people. More than 18,000 people died and hundreds of thousands were left homeless.

 This boy was in a building that collapsed during an earthquake in Turkey. Rescuers dug him out.

Earthquakes and science

Today, people are trying to reduce property loss from earthquakes. Governments are changing the rules for making buildings. Builders are making buildings with layers of rubber. The rubber lets the buildings bend a little instead of falling down.

The cause of an earthquake is usually hundreds of kilometres underground, so humans can't prevent them. But we can reduce the effects by building safer buildings, trying to predict when earthquakes will happen and educating people about earthquake safety.

Governments around the world are changing the rules for making buildings. They want buildings to be built so that they will not fall down during earthquakes.

Predicting earthquakes

Scientists use instruments to find out where earthquakes are likely to happen. A creep-meter measures plate movements. It tells scientists how fast and far plates are moving.

A strain-meter measures stress that builds up as plates get stuck moving past each other. When the stress gets too great, plates can suddenly move large distances quickly, releasing the built up energy. In the 1906 San Francisco earthquake, one plate moved 6 metres in one go.

A **seismometer** measures earthquake vibrations. The vibrations move a pen that scribbles lines on paper called a **seismograph**. The lines tell scientists how big the vibrations are, and by comparing the seismographs from different locations, they can tell exactly where the **epicentre** is.

Scientists also use **lasers** to measure the size of earthquakes. If the Earth moves, so will the reflection of a laser beam. This tells scientists when and how far the ground moves during earthquakes.

 Scientists compare seismographs to find out where an earthquake is.

Before fault movement

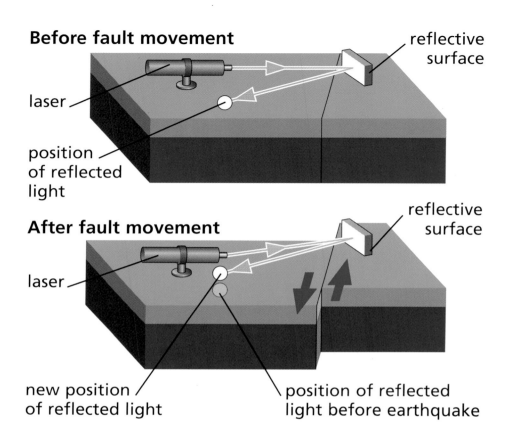

reflective surface

laser

position of reflected light

After fault movement

reflective surface

laser

new position of reflected light

position of reflected light before earthquake

Measuring earthquakes

Scientists use lasers to see how much plates move during earthquakes. The laser is pointed at something that reflects light. The laser moves when the ground moves. Scientists measure how much the reflection has moved to see how much the plates have moved. This system is so sensitive that it could detect the growth of your fingernails. The system is unlikely to help with prediction, but studying the precise movements involved in earthquakes helps us design stronger buildings.

A correct prediction

The best way to prevent deaths would be to predict earthquakes. In 1975, scientists correctly predicted an earthquake in China. They noticed many foreshocks. They believed the foreshocks meant that a large earthquake was coming. The government told about 3 million people to leave the high-risk area. One day later a major earthquake hit. It destroyed many buildings. Thousands of people would have died if they had stayed.

But this is the only example of successful earthquake prediction. One year later, in 1976, 250,000 people died in China when an earthquake struck without any warning. Scientists know how many earthquakes to expect each year based on what has happened in the past. They can sometimes tell what areas are likely to have earthquakes. But they still cannot tell exactly when an earthquake will happen.

More research is now aimed at reducing the effects of earthquakes and saving more lives. Many of the 14,000 people that died in the 1999 Turkish earthquakes would have survived if their homes and offices had been designed and built like the earthquake-proof buildings in California.

Glossary

aftershock small earthquake that happens after a large earthquake

dam strong wall built across a stream or river to hold back water

damage harm that something does

epicentre place where an earthquake starts

fault crack in the Earth's surface where two plates meet

foreshock (FOR-shok) small earthquake that happens before a large earthquake

laser device that produces an extremely narrow and intense beam of light

magnitude (MAG-ni-tewd) strength of an earthquake

plate slowly moving section of the Earth's crust

Richter Scale (RIK-tur SKALE) scale that measures an earthquake's strength

seismometer (SIZE-mo-meter) instrument that measures earthquake vibrations

seismograph (SIZE-mo-grahf) instrument that records earthquake vibrations

tsunami (soo-NAH-mee) huge ocean waves

Addresses and Internet sites

International Seismological Centre
Pipers Lane
Thatcham
Berkshire, RG19 4NS

British Geological Survey Headquarters
Kingsley Dunham Centre
Keyworth
Nottingham, NG12 5GG

International Seismological Centre
www.isc.ac.uk/

British Geological Survey – Earthquakes
www.earthquakes.bgs.ac.uk/

Earthquakes
www.fema.gov/kids/quake.htm

How Earthquakes Work
www.howstuffworks.com/earthquake.htm

Index

Max and Grandma
and Grampa Winky

Danielle Steel
Max and Grandma and Grampa Winky

Illustrated by Jacqueline Rogers

**Delacorte
Press**

Published by
Delacorte Press
Bantam Doubleday Dell Publishing Group, Inc.
666 Fifth Avenue
New York, New York 10103

Library of Congress Cataloging in Publication Data

Steel, Danielle.
    Max and Grandma and Grampa Winky / Danielle Steel ;
illustrated by Jacqueline Rogers.
        p.   cm.
    Summary: Grampa, Mommy, and Daddy help seven-year-old Max
deal with his feelings of sadness and loss following the death of his
grandmother.
    ISBN 0-385-30165-0
    [1. Grandparents—Fiction.   2. Death—Fiction.]   I. Rogers,
Jacqueline, ill.   II. Title.
PZ7.S8143MAV   1990
[E]—dc20   89-77986
                                                        CIP
                                                        AC

Designed by Judith Neuman-Cantor

Manufactured in the United States of America

April 1991

10 9 8 7 6 5 4 3 2

To Omi and Opa, Vovo, Nani, and a
grandmother I never knew. . . .
To Grand Daddy, Kuniko, Grandma Stone,
and Nonna and Nonno,
all of our grandparents we love so much,
and who are so special to us.
      with love,

                    d.s.

This is Max. He's seven years old. He lives in New York. His Daddy is a fireman and his Mommy is a nurse, and he has a little brother and sister who are twins. They are two years old. Being twins means they were born on the same day, and have the same birthday.

But on their birthday they each get a cake and their own presents. Their real names are Charlotte and Sam. But everyone in the family calls Charlotte "Charlie."

Right after the twins were born, their
Grandma and Grampa came all the way from
Arizona to see them. Max calls them
"Grandma and Grampa Winky," because they
used to play a funny game with him when he
was very little, and Grampa Winky always
winked at him.

Grandma and Grampa Winky are Max's Daddy's parents. They used to live in New York, but long before the twins were born, Grampa Winky sold his drugstore on Lexington Avenue. He and Grandma retired and moved to a place called Phoenix, Arizona. It's very pretty and warm there. Max and his Mommy and Daddy and the twins went to visit them in Phoenix last year, on their way to California.

Grandma and Grampa Scott are Max's Mommy's parents. They live in California, right near Disneyland. Max loves to visit them, because going to Disneyland is so much fun.

Max loves all his grandparents, and so do Sam and Charlie. When Grandma and Grampa Winky lived in New York, Max and his Mommy and Daddy used to go to their apartment for Thanksgiving and Christmas. But now they live too far away for Max's family to go just for dinner or a little visit. So when Grandma and Grampa Winky come to New York to visit, it's very, very special and Max gets very excited. He loves seeing them and having them stay with him. Once in a while though, grandmas and grampas can get a little grumpy because they're used to doing things a little differently, or they get tired because they're not used to being around children. When he visits, Grampa Winky always says that the twins make too much noise, but Max knows how much he loves them all anyway. And even if they get grumpy, most grandmas and grampas love their grandchildren a lot. And Max's grandparents sure do. Max can hardly wait to see them.

Max had been expecting Grandma and
Grampa to visit for almost four months. They
promised to come for Christmas, but
Grandma Winky got sick and they couldn't
come. And then it was after Easter.

Max was still hoping they'd come soon, but the day before they were supposed to come this time, Grandma got sick again. Max's Daddy explained that there was a problem with her heart. Her heart had been sick before, but now Grandma Winky had had to miss three visits, and Max was really worried.

For two weeks after that, Grampa Winky
called lots of times from Arizona. Sometimes
he talked to Max, and sometimes he just
talked to Max's Mommy and Daddy.

And then, after two more weeks, there was
a very sad phone call from Grampa Winky.
He called to say that Grandma Winky had
died. She was very old and her heart was
very sick. Max's Daddy cried when he told
him. Max's Daddy was very sad because
Grandma Winky was his Mommy and he
loved her very much, and Max's Mommy
talked about how much they were going
to miss her.

Max was going to miss her too. He used to
love baking cookies and playing hide and
seek with her, and helping her plant flowers
and vegetables in her garden in Arizona.
Grandma had always told him on the phone

how well the carrots and radishes that he had planted were doing. She had promised to bring some with her when she came to New York to see him, but now she wouldn't be coming at all. Never.

He would never see Grandma Winky
again, he thought to himself as he lay in bed
that night, feeling sad and lonely. And then
Max's Mommy came in to talk to him about it.

Max told her how sad he was feeling and how much he missed Grandma and Grampa . . . all his grandmas and grampas. Because if something had happened to Grandma Winky, then something might happen to Grampa Winky too, or even Grandma and Grampa Scott in California.

"Couldn't it?" Max asked his Mommy, sitting up in bed and holding tight to his teddy.

Max's Mommy explained, "Yes, something could happen to any of the grandmas and grampas, because they are a lot older. But all of them are healthy and fine, so there is no reason to think that any of them would have a problem.

"Everyone has to die someday," Max's Mommy continued, "but usually not till they're very, very old. And we believe that one day, after we all get very old and die, then we'll all be together again in a beautiful, happy place called Heaven."

"Will Grandma Winky be there?"

"Yes, I think so." And then Max's Mommy explained, "Different people believe different things about Heaven. But I think that all good people who love each other always stay together, even in Heaven."

For a minute, Max looked happier, and
then he looked worried again. "But what will
Grandma Winky do now, before we all get
there?"

Max's Mommy smiled. "She's probably
making a beautiful garden, and that's how we
have to remember her, with her pretty
flowers and her vegetables. Remember her
delicious chocolate chip brownies?"

"And her pecan pie, and apple pie, and the gingerbread houses she always made for Christmas!" Thinking about all the nice things Grandma Winky used to do made Max feel sad again. But he felt happy, too, because he had so many good memories of his Grandma.

Max's Mommy and Daddy flew to Phoenix the next day to help Grampa Winky make arrangements. That was something he had to do to put Grandma Winky's things away and take care of the garden. Max's baby-sitter, Jean, came to stay with him and the twins. All three of them really liked her.

She was a very, very nice lady, and they always had fun with her. And that night, after Jean put the twins to bed, Max told her all about what had happened to Grandma Winky.

Three days later, Max's Mommy and Daddy came home, and they brought Grampa Winky with them. Max was so happy to see him! At first, Max thought he seemed a little quiet and sad, but after a while Max made Grampa Winky laugh, and they even played the winking game just like they used to.

They talked about a lot of happy things,
and Max was really excited when he saw the
carrots Grampa Winky had brought from
Grandma Winky's garden. They were exactly
like the carrots Max had helped her plant
when he went to Arizona last year.

One day, Max and Grampa Winky went for
a walk in Central Park. They sat for a long
time, watching the boat pond. "You know,"
Grampa Winky said, "we'll always have
Grandma Winky with us in our hearts,
because of all the nice memories she left us."

Max nodded, thinking about her again,
as he slipped his small hand inside his
grandfather's great big one.

"I love you, Grampa," Max said.

"I love you too, Max. And Grandma Winky
loved you too."

"I know." Max smiled, feeling happy again,
as he and Grampa walked home, talking
about Max's next trip to Arizona.